PARENTS,

OUR GREATEST TEACHERS

Author, Alex Balgood

Book Imprint AlexBalgood

Copyright ©AlexBalgood2021

Cover photo or design by Ricardo Alcala

Library of Congress data available upon request.

ISBN: 979-8-9852623-0-8

First Printing, 12/2021

Dedication

I would like to dedicate this book to all children that have, at some point in their lives, realized that their parents were doing their best to raise them, whether that was a little or a lot. We are not here to judge our parents, even when we feel they were the worst, even when they have hurt us or not loved us. Our parents are one of our biggest teachers. If they hurt you, gift yourself forgiveness and love, if they loved you, love your own children and others around you even more.

Life is here to teach us and for us to make the best of it.

Lastly, thank you to my parents. My dad, through his very short life, gave me the love of life to live fully, not through his words but by his way of life. Te extraño, Pa. To my amazing mother, with everything she went through as a younger kid, her rocky life with Dad, and ending up being a single mother of three, taking the role of mom and dad, I thank you Mother for never giving up on life, knowing that always and always, after the storm, there will be that sun, that light, that hope. Te quiero, Ma.

Acknowledgements

I would like to acknowledge all those strangers whose faces and names I may have forgotten, but the smiles and acts of kindness and/or maybe roughness helped me keep moving through life.

I heard Oprah say once that it is important for every single one of us to have someone to regulate our lives, whether it is our friends, co-workers or family. It is important to have those "regulators", those people that listen to us when we are happy or are hurting, those people that hear us at times nagging about the events in life. I would like to acknowledge you and to tell you how important you are for me and for everyone out there, listening, supporting, and loving us. You make people like me better.

Lastly, I'd like to acknowledge everyone that has gone out of their way to teach me and to show me love.

Special Thanks

There are so many people that I need to list and thank for everything, from sheltering me at your home, to feeding me, to letting me lay my head on your shoulder, to everyone that gave me the tough love and pushed me to be the true version of myself. YOU all know who you are!

Thank you to my mentor Laura Michelle, all my guest writers, my best friend and designer Ricardo Alcala, and my friend and sister/best editor Armine Pogosian. My supporter, 2nd editor and friend Kim Ha. This book was made possible because you guys supported me all the way to the end, so thank you!

And lastly to my launching team/friends. All of you that spread the word about this book to friends and on social media.

I love you all and I'm blessed and thankful for all of you.

Table of Contents

"There is no greater agony
than bearing an
untold story inside you."

— Maya Angelou

Introduction

For my whole life, I have praised myself for how independent I am. I was the typical teen that didn't need anyone's help. I lived life my way. At 14, I asked my mother to let me live with my grandparents in The States. My mom was petrified that her little girl wanted to rule her own life, but I feel she knew that with or without her help, I was going to end up doing what I was determined to do. She finally agreed, and that was the beginning of taking the strings of my life into my own hands.

I always saw my parents as being old, outdated, and not knowing fun and what life was all about. Years after the passing of my father, I found myself translating his death certificate for a legal process that I was going through at that time. It was only then that I realized that my father was so young when he passed away; he was only 41! He was full of dreams, he was driven and funny, he did so much throughout his very short life, and I just came to realize all that when I turned 32!

Yes, I was 32.

"Everybody is a genius.
But if you judge a fish by its ability
to climb a tree, it will live its
whole life believing that it is stupid."

- Albert Einstein

Chapter ONE

The Engineer

The coolest thing about being a kid is that titles
are of no importance at all. I grew up in a family of
5 - Mom (The General), Dad (The Engineer), Big
Brother (The Perfectionist), Little Brother (The
Dreamer), and Me (The Curious).

Mom and Dad got married under very non-
traditional circumstances. They were in their 20s.
Mom was homeless at the time, living with friends
and striving to finish her career as a dentist. It was
at that same university that my mom met my dad.
He was well off, coming from a family of 12
siblings, him being the youngest, all of them
educated and graduated from universities.

This is your super cliché story. A well-off young man meets a poor younger woman in school. They fall in love and get pregnant with my oldest brother. She quits school to make money for this new family, because in those days you either have a child or a career. Dad followed as the culture dictates - once you get someone pregnant for whatever reason, the next step is now marriage. He did in fact finish school, marry Mom and try to make things work out.

I'm sure you have perhaps heard your parents' story, right? But honestly, we know almost nothing - not the happiness or sadness that they might have felt, nor their worries or concerns, being that most of our parents got together in their late teens or early 20s. I can definitely say now that the first time I heard their story, I may have been judgy and had the thoughts of "Who's stupid enough to get pregnant or get married at that age? This is crazy!" or "Leaving school to have kids?! That is terrible!" I was about 15 years old then. I didn't know any better.

At the time, there was not a lot of access to the internet, no social media, and no cellphones. You have to put all that into perspective. There was a lot more time spent outdoors - people trying to find new adventures or having conversations face-to-face. They didn't text; they wrote letters. Some of them were sent, and some of them were forgotten. When we talk about our parents' stories in this book, I would like you to put time into perspective, and imagine how different their lives were then.

The first 6 years of my life were amazing. We had
everything: a nice big apartment with beautiful
furniture and paintings on the walls. We had a
maid. We had dogs and ducks (I know, it's a funny
combination), and we traveled to many places.
Vacations were amazing. Mom and Dad took good
care of themselves. Now that I think of it, they
were gorgeous! I thought I had the coolest family,
including my two brothers - my oldest always
bugging me but still being nice at times, and my
baby brother, so fragile and funny. I remember the
clear and crisp air in the house coming in from our
big windows in the apartment we lived in as kids.
My favorite thing was going to the fridge, grabbing
the Greek yogurt, getting the strawberries,
grabbing a bowl, pouring a spoonful of each,
mixing it up, and sitting on the big green reading
chair next to the window facing the front street and
just looking outside as the sun warmed my face.
As I looked outside, looking from the 2nd floor, it
felt awesome. I felt like I could see many things
that others couldn't. Life was good.

Dad graduated as an engineer. To me, he was the
smartest person in the world. Everywhere we
went, people would address him as "Engineer", as
a sign of respect. He carried himself like the
president - or so it seemed to me at the time. He
was nice and always willing to help anyone,
whether it was at restaurants or any place that
would provide any service. He always treated
everyone the same.

Then one day, Dad was no longer at home. Mom never really explained why, at the time. I do remember one day some people came to the house - they were insurance people (not sure their exact title). They knocked at the door so hard I thought they would break it. Mom was so scared. I had never seen her like that. She whispered to me and my brothers to not make any noise. I could tell in her eyes that she didn't know what to do. For the first time, I saw fear in her eyes. She held us tight until those men at the door left. Nothing was said, just a deep silence until they were gone.

My parents got divorced a little bit after that. But what had happened? Well, Dad had an amazing position at the company that he used to work for, and apparently greed took over him. He was part of one of the biggest frauds in his company. When those men came to my house, they were trying to repossess everything that we had. So Dad fled and then moved to a different country. He came back maybe five or six years later. I never found out how his big mistake was resolved.

When he came back, Mom didn't want to know anything about him. He had chosen his path and my Mom had chosen hers, far away from his.

Dad had so many talents. He was always trying to invent something. He was so large in his thinking. He always seemed to have infinite projects - nursery owner, artist, inventor, politician and engineer - always trying to innovate things and make the big bucks. But, he never really did. He struggled. I think back now that every time I saw him, he was in a different house, which as a young kid you think is cool, but reflecting now, it must have been hard for him going from house to house.

When Dad came back, I had already moved out. I was about 16 or 17 years old. When I opened the door at Mom's house, I saw Dad, just standing there, like 50 pounds lighter, greenish looking skin, and the look in his eyes that were saying, "I'm sorry, I love you, and forgive me" all at once. He didn't say anything. I said hello as I slowly moved away from the door. Mom saw me from the kitchen and walked to the door as fast as she could. I probably looked as if I was going to pass out. My youngest brother was there, and he didn't say anything either. Mom walked Dad to the table and they sat down. I can't remember what my mom told him. I have a picture in my head of the two of them seated at the table. It felt as though time was still, while my mind was going wild.

As it turns out, my dad was very sick. We all know that people get sick and die, but this was Dad we were talking about. My mighty dad! The Engineer! The funny, smart, and perfect person that I loved dearly. Nobody had to explain to me what was going on. After the shock settled in, I didn't say anything. I didn't have the skills, the tools to comfort him, to tell him that I loved him, that I admired him, or that I loved all his business ideas. I don't even remember saying "I love you" to him. I guess Mom was so busy working and Dad was too absent all the time to show us how to show appreciation for each other or how to hug or be supportive of each other. I was just a kid and was scared. I had never been as close to real death as that day. I was frozen and started feeling nothing at that moment in life. I had no tools to comfort him or myself. I almost treated the situation as if nothing was happening to him at all. Like it was just a bad dream or nonsensical life event.

After that numbing day, Dad got better for a year or so. I felt relieved. I really thought things were back to normal. But I was wrong. He started to get sicker and sicker, I never knew what to tell him. I was such a great bullshitter, always acting and singing at school, but I always froze every time I saw him. I just didn't know what to do or how to act.

One of the last times I saw him, I walked into his room, bringing with me all my sketches I had been working on. I wanted him to see them and perhaps get distracted from the pain he was feeling or whatever was going through his mind that day. I saw him lying there, just staring into space. I said, "Hi Dad, how are you feeling today?" He turned to look at me and asked me who I was. I tried my best to not run away and cry my eyes out. I didn't move. My feet were stuck to the floor. My chest was so tight that it hurt. I couldn't breathe for a second. I felt like I was standing by the door for hours, like if time had stopped again, just to give me a break from the heartache I was feeling, from the nightmare I was living. I think after losing a loved one, your parents forgetting who you are is a very strong second worst thing to feel, and I was living it all, all at once.

I then took a deep breath, and I said, "Dad, it's me, Alex, your daughter." He took a look at me again and said, "Oh yes, what's going on?" I figured explaining to him that for a second, he had forgotten about me was really not worth explaining. I sat at the foot of the bed. I told him I was excited to show him my new sketches, and I said in an almost crying and broken voice, "I need you to get better because I know soon, I will become a famous painter and I want you to be there. And maybe one day I'll get married and I want you to be there for that too. I want you to know the guys I will be dating." He didn't seem to understand any of what I had just said. He just stared at my drawings and smiled, and shortly after, he fell asleep. I gave him a kiss and left him there sleeping like an angel. That was my last conversation with him.

This year will be the 20th year of his passing. As I'm writing this, I am overwhelmed with all the feelings, processing all those feelings that were stuck for so long. It feels like I'm drowning in my own breaths.

Seeing Dad like that, I felt such an impulse to just leave, leave town, leave far from where this traumatic event was happening. I had some paintings done. I sold most of them and gave away the rest. They were like my babies, and I wanted people to keep them and love them as much as I did. I saved enough money and asked my grandma, who lived in a different country, to let me move in with her for a bit, and she did. I moved, and two weeks later, my dad passed away. I established myself at my grandma's house. I had also gotten a little job at a clothing store. I just wanted to run away from life, from Dad, Mom, my family, my thoughts, everything! That was one very good skill I felt I had. I called myself "a runner", and that's pretty much what I did. I ran away from everything that slightly brought me any emotional discomfort. I would just run.

I remember one of my uncles stopping me as I was heading to work one day. He said, "I'm sorry your dad just passed away." I said, "Ok," and left to work, trying to avoid that whole situation. It was a very gloomy and empty afternoon that day. There were no cars as I walked a few blocks to that clothing store where I used to work. There were no people. Not one soul came into the store. My mind was still. I couldn't think or feel. I was in shock and frozen. It seemed like I lived that way for a few months. I don't remember anything. It was like I was living the same gloomy day with no cars and no people, just dark and ugly days for a while. I spoke very little, almost as if I had run out of words. Nothing was coming out. I started painting again. The smell of the canvas and the paint were my only friends, the only ones that understood me and let me be me. Eventually, I brushed things off and moved on, and I pretty much lived in survival mode for a long time.

At that time, I had no perception of time and age. I just knew that Dad was old, or at least older than me and that maybe old people just die. I couldn't make sense of why it had to be my dad. Why did he have to die? He was such a cool and funny guy. I mean he did do unlawful things, and was not always great with Mom, but he was a good dad or at least he tried when he was with me and my brothers.

Fourteen years after my Dad's passing, I needed to translate some legal documents for my mother, one of those forms being my father's death certificate. At first, I didn't think anything of it. I started the translation process for all the documents. The death certificate was the last one. Subconsciously I didn't want to see it. Finally, I started reading it. His name, last name, cause of death and his date of birth and death, and I immediately did the math. He was only 41 when he passed away! At this point, I'm in my 30s and I started trying to put my parents' life parallel to mine and compare where they were in *their* 20s, 30s and 40s.

In their 20s, Mom and Dad were forced to marry due to the heavy pressure of culture and society. Dad finished school and had an amazing job but decided to get greedy and consequently had to leave his family, his great job, and his wife. My parents were divorced by their 29th birthdays. My mom, in her 20s, had 3 kids and a job. She struggled so much. She had a shitty job. She knew she could offer more to the world. However, being a single mom of 3 was not easy, as she had to work double shifts to have enough money to provide for her family. She hardly saw us. My brothers and I bounced around from aunt to aunt, and grandma to grandma. I had my first love at 23. I pursued art for my career and although it did not make me a lot of money, I didn't care because it made me happy. I hopped from couch to couch, and sometimes even slept in my car. I was living day by day trying to figure life out.

In her 30s, Mom decided to go back to school. Juggling 3 kids, school, and a fulltime job, Mom always tried to give us the best. She eventually graduated as a nurse and went on to do what she always did best - helping others at the hospital every single day. Life felt lighter for her. Although Dad was gone for a few years at that point, in his thirties he was always trying to invent the next best thing in the world and always having a different job. In his late 30s he came to tell us he was sick, he fought as much as he could. He loved life so much. As for me in my late 20s and early 30s, I had just gone through the worst break up, or so I thought. I thought I was going to marry this guy, have kids and be happy forever, but instead was heartbroken for years, I started to read all the self-help books I could find, and all those books kept me going into finally finding my best life.

After seeing both my parents' and my life parallel to each other, it just came to me - this "Aha moment" that overwhelmed me for a while. Having a real understanding of time and where my parents were in time in correlation with my life was such a mind-blowing thought.

Please take a moment and do that exercise yourself for just a second and soak all that in. Where were your parents in their lives at your current age?

"One day you will wake up
and there won't be any more time
to do the things
you've always wanted.
Do it now!"

-Paulo Coelho

Chapter TWO

Turning Point

Dad was dead and I couldn't change it. From that day on, I had a different appreciation for life.

My parents were not old at all. They were full of life, drive, passion for their dreams, and always trying to be better and striving for success. It didn't matter what they had to do, they were willing to do it.

After I realized that, I wanted to change to be better, to have a more meaningful life - a grand life, just like my parents wanted to, and to make a difference in the world. I didn't know how to start. From living in survival mode to actually being present and aware, making a plan, and following the plan. I realized that after I left home in my late teens, I distanced myself from my family - Mom and siblings. I spoke to them maybe once every year, just to say hi. I never said, "I love you" or "I miss you". I think I called just so they wouldn't complain that I didn't call for the whole year. I didn't know who they were anymore. I didn't know Mom or my brothers. I missed out on many big events such as the graduation of my brothers, my oldest brother's wedding and the birth of his child. I missed all those milestones of my little brother.

It was a lot to take in, but I wanted to change the life I was living. Living in survival mode was not bad, I guess. I gained a lot of friends. Were they real friends? I'm not sure, but I loved them like the family I was longing to have. Traveling everywhere was nice, but even then I would always have that thought of "I wish my family could share this experience with me." Living paycheck to paycheck was my normal, art was my escape, and so was dancing. I did many things to cope with the emptiness that I would feel. At times, I would feel it more than other times, but staying busy allowed me to escape. It just kept me going.

One day I stopped and asked myself, "Where do I come from? Who do I act like? Am I more like Mom or Dad?" I suddenly wondered many things about myself - my ways, my likings, my impulsivity, my love for art, and my appreciation for people who provide a service. I wondered about many things. Here I was in my early 30s asking myself who I was. *This is a good moment to ask yourself*

I paused for a minute. I felt a bit stupid asking those questions. At that point I wasn't too sure who Mom and Dad were. I went right away to my friend Marina. She is older than me, and had just graduated as a chiropractor. I wanted to be like her. She seemed to have everything under control. We met initially when I was 19 and now here I was, in my 30s, still trying to make sense of who I was. I give her a lot of credit for my growth. She influenced me in many ways - how independent I was and outgoing and smart. I learned from her that we should never spend what we don't have, a lesson serving me throughout my adult life. I didn't even obtain a credit card till I was 29 because I needed to improve my credit score.

After that quick assessment of who I was, I kept thinking about who else had influenced me? I thought of my Aunt Francis and Uncle Beto. They are an amazing couple full of love and they always treated me as one of their daughters. They used to take care of me if Mom was busy at work. I thought, "I'm sure they had a big impact on the shaping of my personality." After that, I thought about my grandmothers.

My Dad's mom passed shortly after Dad did. She was nice, but a bit of an introvert. When I was at her house, she didn't say much. The only time I remember her talking the most was when I was 11. I had just broken my elbow, so I had to live with her for a bit. Every morning, she would walk with me to school and we would pray together. She also taught me how to sew. Thinking back now, I feel like she only taught me how to do things so I would stop talking. Her perfect day was just to be in silence. She would have me do all these little projects and tasks that would keep me really busy. Maybe now I like to do manual arts because of her. Although I never had an actual conversation with her, she was nice and also fed me the best food. She was full of thoughts and I wish she would've shared them with me.

My mom's mother also took care of me here and there. She fed me and let me watch her cook. She always had crazy stories that never made much sense to me, but she was nice enough to have me in her house at times. One of my memories with her was when I was a kid and we used to have ducks. As they grew, Grandma would say, "They are ready to eat." I was little - maybe 6. I didn't feel scared or shocked, didn't give it much thought. She took the ducks to my aunt's house. She said a little prayer and thanked the ducks for feeding us, just as she would with any other food she would make. She would bless them and then BOOM would crack their necks. I think that that experience has translated now into the respect that I have for nature, plants, and the understanding that some animals are here to feed us. I also know the importance of being thankful for everything that is around us that helps us thrive and be nourished and makes us feel alive. As I reflected, I thought to myself: yes, she fed and took care of me at times, but who she was or where did she come from? I had no clue, and it was crucial information on my quest of finding who I was.

After about 15 years without hanging out with my maternal Grandma, I went back to see her. I was on a quest to find out who she was. It was nice to hang out with her again. She was 80 at that time. I knew she loved plants, so I decided to take her to a different botanical garden every weekend. I was amazed at the amount of beautiful places in town. She enjoyed herself but didn't talk much. I often tried to ask her about her childhood but never got a concrete answer. She would answer most of the time with "I can't remember, it's been so long now." I asked her about what she liked and disliked, but those answers didn't really make sense either. I figured, "Well, who am I to come and interrupt people's lives after so long?" I eventually stopped asking questions, and just decided to enjoy watching her laugh or be amazed by something at the park, or just stare at the birds or the water fountains.

When I was about 34, I started hanging out with Grandma. I took that as an excuse to call my mom and tell her that I had been spending time with her mother. She was just happy to just talk to me after so long. A little while after, I started to Facetime her every day. At first, it was literally like talking to a stranger. Even her face looked different to me from what I remember from when I was a kid. Conversations started as small talk and mostly about the weather. Then I started opening up a bit more about my boyfriend, my friends, and my job. I also started asking questions about her and her upbringings. My Mom was a retired nurse. She was living by herself and enjoyed going for brunch with her friends. I would ask eventually about Dad and when they were together, but Mom didn't like to talk about the past.

Thinking about Dad, I really had to go deep into my memory and think about all the moments I was with him. Some of my best life lessons were from him. He would always say that we have within ourselves everything to be successful, to be anything we want to, and that you don't need school unless you want to be a doctor. Ha, that always made me smile. It just expanded my possibilities. That statement was so infinite and big, I now know for sure that we do - everyone of us - have everything we need to fight and succeed in anything we can think of in life. (*Even if school is on your path, you've got this!*) The way my father conquered each day was so powerful. He would dress in nice clothes, impeccable shoes and had his hair fixed up all the time. He was always ready for his next opportunity, always sharp and in a good mood. I know that I won't be able to make new memories with him, but when I do right by him and live life with such an infinite feeling, where nothing is far, and where all dreams are so tangible that nothing feels impossible, I know he is with me. His grandchildren will know who he was. They will know the good and the bad and how he fought till the end.

**"Everyone needs to be valued.
Everyone has the potential
to give something back."**

- Princess Diana

Chapter THREE

The General

The General, as I called my mother for a very long time, symbolizes the very strong personality and almost scary vibe she had when we were kids. She expected us to get up, fix our beds, clean up, brush our teeth, eat good food only, and get solid "A"s on our report cards, no matter what. We would hear her say, "That is your only job. You must get an 'A'". Her standards were always really high with everything. She was mostly always on the run and trying to get things together at home, especially preparing meals. She would leave food prepared for us, especially when she would take double shifts. We just had to warm it up. She didn't talk much, but when she did, it was mostly to tell us off, like how inconsiderate we were if we didn't pick up after ourselves. We never really went out to restaurants. It was a treat to get food from a food stand near the house. She really tried her best to keep us fed, clothed, and housed. There weren't many conversations nor much physical affection. Plus, most of the time we were at my grandmas' or aunts' homes.

In her own journey to find some peace, my mother experimented with various religions, and with that, we were forced to try them too. All of them were based on fear. If you didn't obey or repent for whatever you did, you would definitely be on the bad side of God. I was in fear of almost everything.

As I grew older and became more outspoken, I felt that she had no say in my life or how I ran it - or so I thought. I was maybe 10 or 11 and thought of myself as a very grown individual. Wow. I resented Mom for a very long time - all those expectations, all those religions. It was our job to be the best, but I never felt any gratification for any of our accomplishments. Birthdays were nice when we were very little, but then as we got older, we'd be lucky to get a cake, if Mom had the time or the money for it. Her mind was too busy trying to give us the best to succeed.

After I left, before the passing of my father, I just wanted to be free to do whatever I wanted. I wouldn't say that I hated my mother, but I just had so much resentment towards her that it made it easy to not see her for about 15 years. I spoke to her sporadically and felt nothing. It seems funny now how all those times that she spanked me, hurt me with her words, ignored me and my successes at times, and all those little moments of disconnectedness and arguments caused by her or me, made me let her go so easily.

Honestly, take a brief moment and think about all those moments where you really wanted a divorce from your parents, because they hit you, they said the wrong thing to you, or in a more serious way, maybe they might have abused you or hurt you physically, mentally or beyond. Know that in any of those circumstances you were not at any fault. All parents have one of the hardest jobs, that one job that no one gives you a manual of how not to fuck it up. Unfortunately, most of our parents have not been given the tools to raise their own kids, whether it is because of ignorance, poverty, trauma or multigenerational fears. Sometimes, that's all they have. But, on the bright side, you can break these bad habits, fears, and generational traumas, by just being aware.

Facetiming Mom every day gave me that opportunity to talk to her and perhaps discover the why and how she got to be like that - almost dry and bitter towards life. I was determined to push myself to do it, to discover where I came from and who came before me. I heard Maya Angelo say, in one of her last interviews, that in order to know oneself, we have to discover and honor those who came before us. It really stuck with me. I know Mom was happy to see me on the phone, and we had short and simple conversations. Little by little, with the years on the phone, we ended up having hundreds of conversations. Sometimes we would agree, and sometimes we had bad and nasty arguments, both of us trying to argue our points of view about lifestyle, religion, family members, my career, or expectations in life. We laughed about funny videos, about old jokes, about my boss's obsession with micromanagement at the office; we laughed about my best friend Esteban and how he reminded me of my youngest brother. Both were so nice and intelligent, but both were always lost when it came down to the opposite sex. In our conversations/debates, I wanted her to understand that I was going to stand up for whatever I was debating, or my beliefs. I wanted to show her that I was a strong woman just like her, and that she had to respect me for that.

I also, for the first time in my adult life, showed her vulnerability. Covid had just stricken the world, and we were in lockdown. But, as an essential worker, I had never stopped working.

When the pandemic started, no one knew what was going on. We just knew that it was bad and that people were dying. It was so scary to drive to work on empty freeways. There was no one in my building but the people that worked at the surgery center. It was such an odd feeling to be out there. It was so surreal. Talking to Mom everyday after work made things easier and a bit more normal, even though she kept me informed of everything that had happened that day on the news - national and international. In one of those instances, I watched a video of a nurse saying that the hospital was full and that people were dying and the medical staff didn't know how to help anymore. They were so overwhelmed, being in the hospital for long hours. But she wanted to thank some people that came by the hospital with signs saying, "We are all in this together," and "Heroes don't always wear capes", and "Thank you for all the healthcare providers." When I watched the video, I felt this feeling of love and unity and felt how thankful this nurse was. It was so moving. The next day I called Mom as usual, and I was telling her about the video and what the nurse said, and I broke down in tears in front of Mom. She got a bit teary-eyed herself and said, this whole situation sucks, but God will keep us safe and she smiled like she was virtually hugging me and comforting me. I had never felt so close to her as I did in that moment.

We kept opening up more about all those times that we hurt each other. I finally became an adult, talking things out. She finally started talking about her childhood. Mom shared with me things that she maybe had not spoken with anyone else in her adult life.

Mom was the eldest of 9 kids and grew up very poor, but she showed character and was whole hearted as a very young kid. Around only 5 or 6 years old, she was taking care of her 4 younger siblings. She would dress them, wash their face, and fix their hair. Grandma did not waste time popping kids one after the other. Grandma was definitely one of many women with no tools to raise her kids. She lived in a room with her 5 kids with one mattress on the floor. Mom remembers that room as humid, cold, scary-looking and smelly. Grandma would leave them there claiming to go work to get money for food. She would leave early and would come back really late. Mom took the role as a mother for her siblings. Sometimes when her siblings were crying because they were hungry, she would walk all of them about 20 blocks to their grandparents.

My great-grandparents didn't have much either but they had a roof over their heads, Great-grandpa was a welder so he would make some money, and Great-grandma was a stay-at-home mom. Keep in mind, my grandma was the eldest of 8. Mom would knock on the big metal fence and her grandparents would let them in and feed them - mostly just beans or rice - and that was their day. Grandma would come get them really late at night, cold and sometimes rainy, waking the kids up. They were crying, not wanting to go back to their house/room. Mom would hear great grandpa telling grandma that it was not good to leave like that from job to job with all these kids unattended. Two of her younger siblings still living with the parents would also tell her off. But Mom lived like that, always trying to help and taking care of the young ones. My mom kept asking grandma to enroll her in school, till she finally did. Mom loved school. It was the only environment where she would thrive with no physical or verbal abuse from Grandma. She would wear second-hand clothes, used shoes, and was malnourished most of the time. Sometimes the only food that she would have for the entire day, was the lunch provided at school.

One night, Grandma came late and was in a really bad mood. Mom woke up and asked her where she had been. Grandma was just not having it. She was not about to be questioned by a 9-year-old kid. She got really mad about it and grabbed her by the arm and kicked her out of the house. It was about 10:00 at night.

Mom was crying, heart broken and so scared. She walked as fast as she could to her grandparents' house. She knocked on the metal fence. Great-grandpa came outside and asked her what had happened. Mom, in tears, told him the story. Great-grandpa saved Mom that night. I can't even imagine a young girl walking 20 blocks in the middle of the night and the many bad things that could have happened to her. Grandma kept on having more kids. But Mom lived with my great grandparents till she was 14 or 15. My great grandpa was my mom's hero. He made her feel seen. Soon after he passed away, Great-grandma and my mom's aunts didn't have enough to take care of her anymore, so she started living on her friends' couches, whoever was willing to let her stay for a while. She was a really good student and a well-behaved girl. So, I'm not surprised so many people were willing to help her. She pretty much took herself all the way to the university - homeless, malnourished, and with the biggest heart. That's when she met Dad.

When they got together Mom was very reserved about having sex. She was totally traumatized about having kids, knowing that for generations that is what happened to the women in her family. But Mom eventually gave in to those hormones and their young love. She, for the first time, felt real love, or so she thought. They got pregnant - definitely not expected. Dad brought Mom to his house where he was living with his mother and 2 sisters. Mom lived with them for a while. She left the university and found a job, and that job gave her benefits, so her delivery was all set. They had the whole wedding dress, tuxedo, wedding at a church, and the reception. That was not mom's life plan, but she accepted it.

As in all families, it is hard to accept others into your circle, and that's exactly what happened to Mom living with my Dad's family, especially because he was the youngest of 12 kids. Everyone was overprotective of him and wanted him to marry someone with a bit more class than my mom. She was marginalized in that house and never felt welcomed. Time passed and she got pregnant again. (All my life I thought I was the middle child, but I was so wrong.) Mom started to have morning sickness again. Dad was super stressed out because his family, especially his sisters, one of them being a nurse, wanted mom to abort the baby. They kept saying that they were still too young to have another child that soon. Mom told them that she didn't want to do that. Mom was scared. That nurse sister took her to the bathroom and inserted some sort of tube in her body. Mom didn't know what they were doing to her, but she knew it was bad. She bled for a while but recovered shortly after. Mom blamed herself for not standing up for herself and her unborn child. She felt that God would punish her. It took her 4 years after her first born child to finally have another child.

Mom told me the story, I could still see the pain in her face as she was telling me the story. At the end, in a very soft voice, almost whispering, she said, "You are the first person I tell this story to." I felt an emptiness in my stomach that hurt. The only thing that came to mind to tell her was that God only gives us what we can handle, and that truly she was a warrior. I don't have kids yet but I can only imagine the pain of losing a kid, even an unborn one, the way she did.

I spent about 15 year without seeing Mom, and very few calls on that timeline. We, as children, spend lots of our time wishing our parents were different, with good reasons or nonsensical reasons. We judge them at times for not making our lives better because we are in need of material things or love.

What I know now is that I knew nothing about my parents. I see now that Mom did her best. Mom wanted her 3 kids to grow up healthy and wanted to provide for us to go to school to have a better future than what she had. Her dream was to be a professional and she eventually made it! She became a nurse in her late 30s. Her oldest and youngest graduated from the university. Her oldest got married and has a beautiful wife and son, and her youngest is still trying to find his voice and place in this world.

The importance of knowing where Mom came from had a huge impact in my life to understand why she turned into this General, wanting everything perfect, wanting us to have nothing other than "A"s in school, and understanding "the why" of her absence when she was working double shifts at work. As a kid I knew she was doing everything for us. She mentioned once or twice that she would hit us with a belt when we didn't do well at school or didn't have the house neat. She really tried her best to give us everything that she didn't have.

Knowing where our parents come from really gives you a different insight of "the why" they scream, "the why" they don't hug or say "I love you" often. It gives you "the why" they are addicts or violent, "the why" they are absent. It gives us the understanding of the WHY of their pain. As there is not a manual for parents, there is also not one for being a good son or daughter, so be kind to yourself. We do hurt our parents as much as they hurt us sometimes, but breaking those chains - that's where we are born again, where we get to start all over.

**"Discipline is helping
a child solve a problem.
Punishment is making a
child suffer for having
a problem.
To raise problem
solvers, focus on solutions,
not retribution."**

- L.R. Knost

Chapter FOUR

The General's Mom

As I came to understand Mom, and some of her "why"s, I felt lighter. I felt the understanding that sometimes, in some situations, our loved ones don't have the capacity to understand life to its fullest. They don't have the capacity to love us the way we would like them to, and that they perhaps don't have the tools. And at that point, we must meet them where they are.

So now I knew Mom's pieces of her difficult story, and I knew I needed to go back a little bit more. That brought me to my grandma - Mom's mom.

She was the eldest of 8, from what I can make of the stories from family members and herself.

She was one of those kids in school that would defend her younger siblings. Fist first, she was tough. She knew at a very young age that she would protect her siblings, even if that meant for her to get in fights at school. She used to love to play marbles and would win every time. I do remember a sad story that she mentioned once to me. She mentioned that when she misbehaved once, Great-grandpa would grab her hands and place them on a hot grill. Was that story true? Maybe. A lot of people in the poor class didn't know better, especially when it came down to raising kids. Violence was not uncommon. She said that after that, she tried her best to be an obedient daughter.

The way I made sense of all these stories, where sometimes Grandma was the hero, and sometimes the villain of the story, is that most of the time we face situations where we act with fear, and a survival mood is a real thing.

I think my grandma at a very young age was bright, street smart, curious and wanted to learn everything she could. She only made it to the 4th grade. She barely knew how to read, write and do some math. Great-grandparents didn't have much. I feel that maybe when you are the eldest of your siblings, parents tend to expect you to help with the siblings and mostly everything, which she did. The only thing is that when you are a curious individual, your mind wonders about everything. You want to try, touch and recreate things that you think are cool. But Grandma, at a very young age, was hit or screamed at. She was taught to be a submissive woman that needed to help men, mostly.

In her one and only relationship, she started having kids in her late teens, with a man that didn't love or respect her as a woman most of the time. She had 9 kids, one after the other. They never married and they were never in love. She never really had an actual job, but instead she just hustled - from cleaning houses, to making food and selling it on the streets. She would talk about the time that she cooked for a high position politician. She also mentioned that she met a few famous singers while working as a cook when she was younger. In my eyes, I think she hustled for her freedom. Maybe her vision was no kids, or at least not as many as she had. Maybe she just wanted freedom to find herself, exploring what school had to offer and/or maybe the arts. She never had the permission or opportunity to be free, to speak up for whatever it was that she wanted to do in life.

The capability to live in her eyes was not an option and not her fault. The place where you are born and the people that surround you have lots to do in how your life might end up. I once tried to interview her about her life and her likes and dislikes. She had no answers. She just stared a deep stare. It didn't matter how I asked the question, there was no answer. Even when

I asked, "What would you like to say to your kids?" there was a profound silence. I know for a fact that she was not a perfect mother. I mean, she did kick my mother out of her house when my mom was only 9 years old. But was she evil? Was she the worst person in the world? I'm sure for my mom, Grandma was all that. But taking a step back, you can see that her own life was so complex, with no guidance. Maybe she also never felt love from her parents, never really found self-love and only found a little love from the touch and words from Grandpa was just enough for her. That was perhaps the most love she knew and that's exactly what she gave to her kids.

Grandma, to me, is someone that I love watching cook and do gardening. Whether all her stories were real or not, I loved her talking to me when she did. Grandma passed on to me the love for nature, for the trees and plants. Grandma took care of me at times. She was not the most nice, even loving, but I think she tried her best. She did all she knew.

As she grows older, I believe she is now 84, her kids have taken the responsibility to care for her, or at least they all try. I hope that by the time she leaves this world, she will be able to say "I love you" and "I'm sorry" to all her kids, including my mom.

Knowing a little about Grandma made me understand the relationship between Mom and me - so much about our anger and frustration in life and towards life. We unconsciously carry things from generation to generation; some of these things, if you want to get into detail, are passed on even at a cellular level. This is some quantum real nerd shit that would be crazy to explain, but the bottom line is that there have been lots of studies that prove that that's what really happens from generation to generation. We pass on traumas and feelings. If we don't talk about our shit, if we don't heal what happened to us, we will continue to pass that to the next generation.

Doing the work has not been easy at all, but it has been really worth doing. Knowing who you really are comes first by knowing who came before you and honoring the good and the bad.

I am grateful to have known my grandmother and my great grandmother - four generations at a table. What a treat! I wish I would have the knowledge to have appreciated this.

Take a minute to think about your grandparents, great grandparents (if you were lucky enough to have met them), and also your parents. Take this moment to see all the bad and the good (habits, thoughts, beliefs, feelings), breathe in all those good feelings, all those happy moments, and breathe out all the bad, the fights, the misunderstanding, the way we wanted them to love us and to make us feel seen. Let go and know that they did as much as they could and the best that they knew.

"Be a loner. That gives you time to wonder,
to search for the truth.
Have holy curiosity.
Make your life worth living."

- Albert Einstein

Chapter FIVE

The Curious

My quest perhaps was not to go back and dig for something, but in doing so, I realized that I was who I was because of all the situations I lived through - all those roads that I crossed, with the people that eventually became friends and with those friends that became family, and with all those individuals that we get to call family, those that sooner or later we realized that for the most part won't disappear from our lives, if we don't want them to. We have their unconditional presence in our lives.

Read the quote below, breath in and find your happy place for a moment:

"Curiosity is a quality related to inquisitive thinking, such as exploration, investigation, and learning, evident by observation in humans and other animals. Curiosity is heavily associated with all aspects of human development, which derives the process of learning and desire to acquire knowledge and skill."

- **Wikipedia**

Curiosity is in all of us and is a natural state. We live and thrive with this power of wanting to discover what this life has to offer. As we grow older, as the Master Don Miguel Ruiz (Author of *The Four Agreements*) said, we start believing in statements and agreements from past generations that limit us from the infinite individuals we can become. Kari Norley (Author of *The Wealthy Alchemist*), in a conversation on "Leap of Health" podcast, talked about the effect of a glass ceiling metaphor used to represent an invisible barrier that prevents a given demographic from rising beyond a certain level in a hierarchy and how we have these hidden obstacles within ourselves that again limit our lives to advance in all aspects. Curiosity is such a big part of everyone's life, yet at a very early age, we start to eliminate it from our daily lives.

I remember being 4 or 5 years old and in kindergarten. My friends and I would play outside at the playground, digging in the garden looking for bugs, and playing in the dirt. I remember being so fascinated by worms and the way they moved. Once, I saw one of my friends cutting one of the worms in half with a leaf. After he did, both pieces of the worm kept moving. It was such an amazing discovery at that time! We thought that the worm could keep living everytime we cut it in half. Whether that was true or not, our minds were so blown. Curiosity and inhibition were our superpowers.

Kindergarten really started to shape my life. I remember I would sit by myself doing puzzles while the rest of my class would be doing something else. Later, Mom told me that I was a bit more advanced than the other kids and in order to keep me quiet and entertained, I was given puzzles because they were the only thing that would keep me from disturbing the class. Just after kindergarten, my superpowers started to dim. I'm sure everyone has a story where adults decided to not see you and your potential but rather dimmed the infinite person you were supposed to be.

I was 15 when I told my mom that I wanted to move out, and the farthest I could go was with Grandma. But, I was not happy there either. All I wanted to do was discover the world. I was about 19 when I moved out of Grandma's house. I lived on friends' couches for a while.

Around my 21st birthday, I moved in with my first boyfriend. I thought he was the one, and you guessed it! He was not. A couple years later, we broke up. I cried for months, and as everyone who has gone through a breakup knows, that pain at that moment is the worst! You feel like life is over and that life has done you wrong. But, I survived. Four months later, I stopped crying and got with someone else.

After that painful breakup, I wasn't sure how to live anymore. Most people think that you meet your partner, fall in love, get married and live happily ever after. But life is definitely not that. That was the first moment I had to stop and really dig deep into who I was and where I was going. Where was my curiosity at that moment? I became homeless for a while, sleeping in my car. And yes I know what you are thinking: "Why not go back to Mom or Grandma's house?" Well, my pride was heavier than that and my ego was through the roof.

Many years later, I learned that asking for help was and is an act of courage. We have everything we need to succeed and grow and to fly as high as we want. We just need to ask. No one is alone! Yes, you read that correctly. You will be so surprised on how many strangers right now are willing to help you, including your blood-related family, if you are lucky enough to have them. And last, but not least, your friends.

In my early 30s, I had a health scare. I went to the emergency room, and they kept me there for almost 4 days. I had never really sat on the thought of dying before then. At first, I was mad with the thought of dying because I knew deep down inside that I was supposed to do more than just being upset about life not turning out the way I wanted. There were things I longed to have, a career I dreamed of, the dream relationship I kept fantasizing about. We are all going to die, but most of us refuse to think about it, to really know what that means for each of us, to know how that thought feels through your skin.

My curiosity, my superpower, kept me alive. Looking at those hospital room walls, and hearing my heart beat for 4 days, brought me back to Mom, Dad, my siblings, and Grandma. Death is such an individual experience. Here I am panicking and refusing to die, but maybe in the next room there is a person in peace and resignation to move to whatever death is. For 4 days, I dwelled on the idea of being gone. The last day in the hospital I woke up, took my monitor and walked to the window facing a small park and I was just an observer of life. I looked at the sky in awe. I watched the trees moving. I stared at the building and acknowledged the cold floor under my feet. I heard the monitor as a life song, just as the soundtrack of that moment. It took almost dying and four days in silence to realize that death is a fact for all of us.

It took a while, but healthwise I got better. My attitude towards life definitely became different. I didn't let my stage fright get to me as bad as before. My panic attacks before a public event got better. I'm glad a glimpse of my superpower kept me going through life. Growing up, shifting from house to house, living through a health scare, overcoming fears that for many are dumb or are an illusion, for me were/are very real, but still I keep working on them. I need to if I want to live fully.

Making peace with death made me live in a different way, I knew every day that if that was my last day, I would definitely leave this word smiling, knowing that until then I did my very best - whatever that meant.

Take this moment to ask yourself:
If I would die in 2 minutes from now, how would that feel? Do you have any regrets? Do you wish to have done more in your long or short life? Did you love enough? Did you find yourself, God, and/or the true meaning of life? Sometimes just being aware of how death might look for you will change the perspective on the simple AND not so simple things in life.

**"A mentor is someone
who allows you to see
the hope inside yourself."**

— Oprah Winfrey

Chapter SIX

The Mentors

Not having Dad around much, then his passing and having Mom being absent and missing moments from my and my siblings' lives, I was blessed to have some great - not "role models" - but what I call REAL models, like Aunt Francis and Uncle Beto. They were amazing and loving to me, not perfect by any means, but they made me feel seen, and loved. They made me feel super important. I guess that is the meaning of being present to others.

Throughout my whole life, I have encountered lots of "Mentors" that maybe at the time didn't seem that way, but now I'm grateful to have encountered those great AND not so great people (I call those the "Hidden Mentors").

Growing up, one of the people that had some of the biggest impacts on my life was my uncle. He owned a printing shop and would give me and my younger brother money after school to buy snacks. I never had a conversation with him, just "Hi Uncle!", "Thank you Uncle!", and "Bye Uncle!" But he was nice towards us. Watching him work at the print shop after school made me feel like I could one day have a business of my own.

Another mentor, my Uncle Noe, kept showing me with his life that dreams come true. He came to the states in his early 20s in search of the "American Dream". He now owns a few properties, has a beautiful family, and keeps on making business.

My art teacher in 7th grade would always push me to do bigger projects. She really believed in me as an artist.

 Another mentor was my instructor in 9th grade for JROTC (Google it and it'll make you smile). He pushed me to be the best, and that year I got an award for the Honor Cadet of the Year.

All of my dance coaches really changed my life. I never knew I could dance. When I decided to start training, I was one of the worst dancers. But there were a lot of coaches that kept me going, and I was blessed enough to go out in the world and compete in some of the biggest dance stages at the time. I even traveled around the world to perform and compete!

There's no doubt that friends and coworkers have had an impact on my life, and of course Mom and Dad and my siblings. They have all become my mentors - directly and indirectly. Have you heard of the saying, "Dance like nobody's watching"? I think we all unconsciously are always watching for those amazing moments that we can treasure of what others teach us, of how others make us feel and how others make us see magic within ourselves.

And let's not forget those "Hidden Mentors" - those kids that pushed us in school, that made us fall and scratch our knees, all those young loves that made us hurt, that gave us those real heartaches, those friends that betrayed us, those family members that were never there when we needed them, those coworkers that made our lives miserable and then there are those drivers that cut us off in traffic. They have ALL had an impact on our lives, no matter how big or how small.

As I mentioned earlier, I've been lucky enough to encounter many wonderful people along my journey who have impacted my life in one way or another. I asked them to reflect and share a bit about their journeys. The following stories are from 8 of these amazing people that had

the courage and kindness to share their stories.
Enjoy!

Angeles, 15, female

Looking back to when I was younger, I would describe my dad as a monster because of all the things that happened. Describing him now that I've grown up a bit, he isn't that bad, although he does lose his temper every once in a while, and we don't really have a good relationship per se. He's ok.

My mom passed away from the most aggressive breast cancer when I was 5. She used to take care of me since my mom and dad were separated. So, it's just been me and my dad ever since my mom passed away. It was my dad that has made me struggle the most. As a kid I remember I was so used to having my mom help me with homework and be there when I needed help with anything. When she passed away, I was lost and I didn't know what to do. So I wouldn't do my homework until he came home so he could help me. When he would get home and saw that my homework wasn't done or I misbehaved, he would hit me and we would go to sleep very late because his patience was - and still is - very short. This continued all the way to 7th grade. I grew up with anxiety, depression, and mentally unstable which led me to self-harm - cutting in this case.

I would self-harm because I didn't have anywhere else to put all my emotions.

A few years later, I've come to learn that violence was never the answer and was never supposed to be an option to begin with. Everything that I went through, all those pushed down/hidden emotions, forced smiles, faking happiness and many other things, made me try and become an optimistic person.

My dad has always been overprotective of me, since I'm an only child and a girl. I remember when I was in middle school I had a friend. We were really close, basically inseparable, at some point she began to smoke the devil's lettuce. I didn't say anything to anyone because I didn't want her getting into serious trouble. I was blinded by the image of our friendship. I didn't realize it was affecting me in a way. When my dad found out, he was calm about it and talked to me about it. He told me how it was wrong and unhealthy for her and me too. I didn't want to believe him because she was my "best friend". Eventually, he decided to move me to another district. At the time, I saw it as something that was completely unforgivable - taking me out of my environment and placing me in an unknown place with unknown people. Looking back at it now, I realize he made the right choice taking me out of a toxic and harmful environment. As a teenager, I find myself keeping all to myself, not sure I have the tools or know the way yet to tell my dad the truth about how I really feel about him...the truth hurts but it's honesty and I will eventually talk to him about all this.

I've already lost my mom, so thinking about losing my dad would make me feel a bit sad sometimes. He's my dad, and I grew up with him. But after a while, I could let go. A lot of people make it sound hard, but when you've had to let a lot of people go in your life, it gets easier as time goes on. I would be a liar if I said I never held onto my dad while going through something. It was when my mom passed away, I cried and my dad held me to try and tell me everything was gonna be ok. I'm trying to understand Dad and how he has dealt with life since Mom passed and the huge task of raising a young girl like myself.

If I could have my mom back for one day, I wouldn't know where to start. I would tell her everything that's been going on during school, new friends I've made, any guys that I like or have asked me out, etc. Having mom gone has been hard, and I am still learning how to cope with her absence.

Mandy, 29 adult female

First, I would like to describe the 3 most important people in my life: my grandma, my grandpa, and my foster dad.

My grandma growing up was always stern and emotional. She showed her love by protecting me the best way she knew how. She believed in rough love but always had it in her heart to spoil me. She knew my mother could not provide for me so she wanted to give me the best life possible. She did. Years later she still has that type-A personality and emanates protection even though she is far. I know I would not be alive if it weren't for her.

My grandfather is definitely a character. Growing up he was always a jokester and tried to teach me lessons through letting me fail (polar opposite of my grandmother). He loved classical music and would play it so loud it would echo around the house. He would always make the most silly faces and bring me joy through telling jokes. To this day, he is still such a jokester and a light-hearted human. I enjoy learning from his wisdom and benefiting from the free oil checks he does, haha.

The final is my foster dad. One of the most selfless and kind people I have ever met. The epitome of his existence is serving others and doing what he can to make everyone around him happy. He's been through so much and yet is still this strong amazing person. The world needs more dads like him. I am very blessed to have come across him and even more blessed that he was my father figure growing up. We don't talk as much anymore, but I still think of him often and am thankful that he saved me.

My mother was the one who made me suffer the most. Growing up was not the easiest childhood. When you have traumatic experiences as a child, they're amplified by 10,000. With the lack of knowledge and experience of the world, every moment is your whole world.I was not so fortunate with the mother I had; but that's okay. In retrospect, everything happens for a reason. The instance that pops to the forefront of my mind is when she pulled me off stage at my singing recital. She and my grandma do not get along whatsoever. My grandmother showed up to my recital and my mother was furious. She walked on stage while I was singing and pulled me off in front of hundreds of students and parents. She was grabbing my wrist so hard it started to bruise. A moment passed where she loosened her grip and I broke free and ran back into the school. I found a teacher and they hid me in a classroom. I was shaking in fear; I thought she was going to kill me, or at the very least, hurt me. CPS was called by 3 people that night. Two parents who witnessed it and the teacher who reported it. Little did I know, that moment triggered the beginning of my foster care journey.

I didn't understand it then, but looking back at my life, I am very thankful for all of the hurt and trauma. Because of it, I can now better navigate situations that come my way that closely resemble anything I've already been through. I'm stronger now than I was then. It was truly a "trust the process" type of journey. I'm thankful for all of it. When I take in foster kids one day, I'll be able to show them the type of unconditional love I wish I had had. In the end, it all works out for the greater good and I have to trust that everything I have been through gave me a purpose for something bigger.

When I was 19, something very traumatic happened to me and I felt like my whole world was falling apart. The only person I ever shared this with was my foster dad. He ended up sitting me down and telling me his testimony in grave detail and then explained to me how he got through it and how he kept hope. This was one of my most impactful experiences with him. He created a space comfortable enough for me to share my experiences and he trusted me enough to share his own. He handled it the best way a parent could. Neither of us were okay, but we made it okay because of how vulnerable we were able to be. He let me know I was not alone and created a safe space for me. I hope to do the same one day for my own children.

My foster dad made me the happiest. He was my best friend. He taught me that there truly is a balance between being a parent and a friend. I can only hope to be half the parent he was one day. I truly value how honest we were with each other. We didn't keep secrets and I truly knew I could go to him for anything and it was the same for him.

He walked me down the aisle on my wedding day. And the look in his eyes just seemed so proud. He had accomplished everything he could've as a parent and it was so telling. I will always be thankful for him. In the times I was in terrible foster homes or wondering if my life was even worth living, he took me in and saved me. He made me feel like my life had a purpose. He took me to church. He shared his experiences and wisdom. He put himself in my shoes and empathized. He was a guardian angel sent from heaven and gave me motivation to keep pushing myself. And for that, I owe him my life.

In all of the chaos in my life, I am truly thankful for the good and bad parents. If it were not for my mother, I wouldn't have met my foster dad. If it were not for my mother, I wouldn't have had my two amazing grandparents raise me. The good balances the bad and without them all, I would not be alive or where I am today. Life is about balance and I can only be thankful for every experience I've had and every parent that I've lived with.

The only advice I'd give to parents would be to let children make mistakes. The best way of learning is failing and trying again. Nothing in life is going to be perfect. Nothing in life is going to be easy. And it's better to prepare your kids for tough lessons while they're young as opposed to sheltering them and then they struggle in the real world.

I would also say that I am so incredibly thankful for the parental figures I've had in my life - blood related or not blood related. They all did an amazing job raising me and loving me unconditionally even when I was a brat or the best child. They all supported me and believed in me even in moments I didn't think I would make it. They're my saviors and guardian angels. Every moment, good and bad, has all led me to this moment and there's no place I'd rather be.

Anthony, 32, male

My mother and father were extremely young and really were not prepared to be parents. By the time I was 2 years old, my father was involved in a car accident that left him brain damaged. My mother was not really emotionally available to be a mother and I was going back and forth between living with my grandparents until that became permanent at the age of 4. I had a lot of different caretakers growing up, even to a point where I grew up speaking Spanish. My father at this point has passed away, and my mother seems to still be living out the same pattern and is doing her best to improve.

I would say my mother is the one that has made me suffer the most. Looking back, it all starts with her being emotionally unavailable and choosing to leave me with my grandparents to go and start a new relationship. It really left me with this feeling of not being wanted. Also, allowing me to witness the domestic abuse that she and my step-father would commit against one another and having that imprinted on my subconscious did not provide for a safe environment and made me seek external things such as food for comfort. My mom chose to drag me into her mess that she was swimming in with another man who later became my step-father. I do feel that not receiving the love of my mother directly has left me seeking the love and validation of another person because her pattern of seeking love in another person instead of loving herself has been brought into my world to clear. It's really given me so much to break through and it's been quite a difficult journey. I still feel as if those lessons are being presented to me as I really step into the depths of what it means to truly love yourself without the approval of any other person.

My grandparents would be the ones that really allowed me to be joyful and feel the depths of these emotions. They were extremely loving and supportive and allowed me to experience my childhood with so many great experiences. They allowed me to experience so many different sports and opportunities through life. And at the same time because they always allowed me to experience life and give me what I wanted, it's been difficult to provide those experiences for myself because I wasn't necessarily taught how to obtain that for myself. It was always given to me. I hold so much gratitude in my heart for my grandparents. Being with my grandparents really allowed for me to receive the love that I needed to be nurtured as a child and has helped shape me into the kind loving soul that I am today.

My mother was a weekend warrior and in and out of my life. Had I not gone to her house on the weekends maybe I wouldn't have been put in situations that are not fair for children to witness - like domestic abuse between partners. I feel like I wouldn't have been able to see the contrast of what wasn't supposed to happen in relationships. So I am grateful for what I have seen because it's nothing that I will ever put my family through.

Honestly, I would say just holding faith in knowing that everything is going to turn out okay regardless of the storm that you may be facing is what got me through. Faith was something that was strongly taught by my grandparents and sometimes it can be difficult to hold faith through a storm.

If I could have my grandfather for a day after he has been gone for 13 years, I would like to just spend time in his presence and let him know how grateful I was for everything that he was able to teach me as I was growing up. I don't know if there is anything I would specifically ask him. I honestly just miss the energy that he provided and would love to spend time within that essence that he provided while he was here on earth.

If I could say one more thing to my parents and grandparents I would say that I love them and I would thank them because I know that they did the best that they could with the lessons that they were able to learn. I have learned to fully accept what I received from those that were my parental figures and I know that I am the only one that has the power to change it.

Marina, 47, female

I'm a healer, a doctor. I was blessed to have the most amazing, loving, caring, down-to-earth parents ever. My family is small and very tight. My grandparents immigrated and left violence and lack of freedom to have the "American dream" and a better future for her two daughters, one of them being my mom.

Both of my parents are unfortunately gone now. They battled chronic illness till the end, but both fought like real warriors till the end.

I honestly cannot remember even one unpleasant moment with my parents. I only think that I would have benefitted if they taught me a bit more about being disciplined. They were super nice, and what else can you expect coming from a communist country, where life was nothing like New York.

Both made me joyful. My mom was sweet and loving, and my dad was funny and protective. I wish I still had them around because it was only when I was closer to 30, when I started really connecting with them as an adult and really enjoyed sharing life with them and asking for their advice.

I think years later, after all the joyful moments, it is an ingrained part of me. I am like them in many ways and enjoy feeling those memories and the pleasant moments. I miss them so much.

It's very sad and lonely without them. Nothing and nobody can replace the feeling of having your parents in your life. It's like a part of you is missing forever.

I think one of the biggest things I remember from my dad is how he reacted to the men in my life. I knew by his reaction and advice who is a real man and is good for me and who is not. The biggest lesson I learned from Mom is that she showed me the definition of unconditional love and how not to be afraid to be who I am, no matter what anyone else thinks.

If I would have one more day with my parents I would of course tell them how much I love them and how important they are to me. I would also apologize to my mom for not being the easiest teenager.

Life has taken my parents - my best friends - but I'm thankful for all of it. I have such a different perspective of life having the smartest and most beautiful daughter to show her how amazing her grandparents were and the legacy they have left me.

Ngocvan Nguyen (Van), 59, female

Both my parents were very strict, old-fashioned, and difficult. Even when I got older, they were still strict but a tiny bit easier. I remember when I was in school if I misbehaved. The school would call Mom and I knew that by the 3rd time, Mom would beat me. Father was financially responsible for the family. Mother made all the familial decisions. I would say Mother was tougher because she was more involved in what my siblings and I would go through in school. My mother wanted the best for us. Physical discipline was big, whether it was a simple waking up late for school or something major happening at school, beating us was the way Mother knew to discipline us

Even though the beating was not ideal, I learned hard work and lots of discipline. I still do not agree with the severity of the punishments from Mother. Violence is never the way, but when you grow up in Vietnam and the midst of war, generations carry that unconsciously home.

Both parents made me equally happy. One of my favorite things we did was the monthly restaurant excursions with the family. All cultures share a love for bonding over food, and that was my favorite as a kid.

I have learned to be self-dependent and to be friendly. As I got older, I can understand why my parents did what they did and why they did. Both of my parents have passed now. I don't know what I would say to them if I were to have them for one more day. It is too hard for me to even think of them. I love and miss my parents.

Ashley, 36, female

I am an only child. My parents were always extremely loving and always put me first. They still do to this day. I am very blessed. My parents are very hardworking and supportive. They always encouraged me, with my dreams of being an artist and dancer, to move away to a different city to pursue my dreams.

I was asked if any of my parents made me suffer. "Suffer" is a strong word. I don't feel that I ever suffered. I think times have been tough and there are moments that have made us stronger. My mom was always overprotective, so it took a lot of effort on my part to help her open her mind. She always did the best she could and I know it was her way of trying to keep me safe.

I have learned so much about who my parents are as humans versus just my mom or dad. I have taken such a great perspective to see who they are separately from their title to me to see how and why their life has shaped to be as it is now. When you are young, you don't always understand why your family is the way it is. I think when you take the time to see who they are as people rather than as your mom or dad, you are able to understand them better. This has helped me in my choices and compassion for them.

Both of my parents made me joyful and happy in their own ways. I love that, no matter their ages, they are both silly. They are not so serious and love to joke around, no matter what life throws at them. They also keep tradition for holidays which always brings us together.

I have learned there will be no other love like my parents love for me. It is interesting. I have searched for this love in a partner and have never found it because I don't think it will exist. A partner can love you in a different way but will never compare to the unity my parents have created for me. I am so lucky to have so many wonderful family memories and traditions to pass along to friends and maybe to my own family someday.

I really do not even want to consider the fact that one day they would be gone. They have always been my rock, my support, my everything. I never hated them nor have spent more than 1 week not speaking and connecting. I think I would be a completely different person without them and I truly dread when this day comes. I pray that I have support around me.

The one teaching that would stay with me forever, and especially I feel the last two years, has happened daily. There have been constant trails for me and I have been very exhausted trying to navigate life and what is next for me. The strongest one that comes to mind is "tutto passe" which means "Everything passes" or "This too shall pass". Nothing lasts forever, you must keep going and remembering these words when faced with a trial. This mindset has saved and allowed me peace even for just a moment.

I would like to say to both of them that you have taught me, shaped me, understood me, encouraged me, filled me, lifted me and done everything possible to make sure I have a wonderful life. I can never repay you for this and I am extremely grateful for the love and dedication to being so selfless. I am so grateful for your consistency in my life. It truly has been the only thing that has carried through life's extreme trials. You always gave me wings to fly. I know so many people who do not have relationships with their parents for whatever reason. I know I am truly one of the lucky ones. Thank you for choosing me.

Nii Ashitei Tetteh, 41, male

My parents raised all 7 of us in a good cop/bad cop style. As a kid, it wasn't that they were strict per se, but there was definitely a regimented bringing up. Bedtime was always 7pm. We had a schedule when school was on holidays - from 7am to 7pm. But we were also allowed to play and watch cartoons on Saturday mornings. My mom was a K-12 teacher, and my dad an engineer. We definitely became our mom's projects with after school tutoring and tutoring before we even got to school age. But it wasn't all cartoons and weekend potlucks with our international neighbors. My grandad was an old-school disciplinarian, meaning he believed in corporal punishment, and my mom was a righteous advocate of this, while my Dad had little stomach for it. At one point, it was bad enough that I packed a bag to run away and realized we were living in the middle of the desert in Saudi Arabia (we moved there when I was 2 or 3 years old). Corporal punishment and push to achieve academically was everything to

Mom ("the key to a good life", and why would she not want that for her children?). And it wasn't just me, it was all 7 of us!

My mom was the nurturer AND also the punisher and dominant figure in the house since she gave up her career (women in Saudi Arabia could not work at the time). I don't think my mom has ever quite realized the impact of her words and actions on us. I remember a time I had strep throat and didn't say anything to my parents because I was always getting in trouble. That infection shut down my kidneys and led to a 3 month stint in the hospital with my mom sleeping on the floor beside me. But another time, my mom found me, after a bad day of bullying at the American International School, in the bathtub filled with washing detergent with a bottle of bleach next to me. I was picked on for being dark-skinned and wanted desperately to become lighter-skinned. I had rarely ever seen her so alarmed. During the Gulf War in 1990, Dad had to join the military and we (my mom and the kids) moved to Ghana. After being in a school where there were only 5-6 black kids out of 1,200, I now realized that there was an ENTIRE CONTINENT of people that looked like me. It was at that point that my coming of age moment occurred.

I would say my relationship with my mom has been complicated, at the very least. At a point, there was a lot of hate and resentment and just wanting to get out of the house, out and away from her. But like I said, it was also complicated. My dad, on the other hand, was always a constant - he didn't talk much, and he let us live our life and experience our own experiences. When we would get whipped by Mom with a cane or sometimes a belt, Dad would take us out for a long ride in his car or take us to the store to get chocolates. My parents did old school parenting - he let my mom take care of the house and kids, and he worked to provide and make sure we went to good schools, had good food to eat and got to see the world we lived in (vacation homes in Ghana, in Egypt and the Mediterranean). My dad is now 81. He lived with my brother and me since mid-2015; I'd seen him at college graduation in 2002 and at my older brother's wedding in 2014, but it really hit me how quickly he had somewhat wasted away by doing nothing - in the sense that he had stopped being active and doing things. He could simply stay home to drink and watch TV all day, day after day after day.

The first thing that comes to mind, when I think of my past struggling moments in life with my parents, other than being forced to eat custard (gag), tapioca pudding, and Fruit Loops cereal (I'll never eat Fruit Loops again), was the corporal punishment for everything and anything that didn't meet Mom's expectations of intelligence, attention or what she had asked us to do. Needless to say, I do not believe in corporal punishment as an SOP, or standard operating procedure. There is no such thing as raising any two children the same way because we are all different.

I spent years burying my sensitivity to the point where I didn't know and I couldn't tell you how I felt about things because it took a while for the impact to get to me. Because we learned out of fear of the cane and caning, you had to put all that emotion aside because it only got you more lashes. Years later, I would say my upbringing made me resent violence towards children. Yes, children can be all over the place, and yes sometimes it can teach, BUT we have to be VERY CAREFUL as a society what we do with it on a personal level, because it can really profoundly impact someone and not in a good way.

After everything I went through, my relationship with my parents really taught me about a mother's undying love and a father's dedication and steadfastness. In a strange way, their relationship taught me about harmony (my first memory is of them dancing in the living room). Now, I LOVE dancing and it has always been close to my heart. I believe there is a pure quality to people that comes out when they dance. I think perhaps because we grew up somewhat isolated, dance gave me a desire to meet people and find out what they are all about.

Bogin, 55, male

When I was younger, I looked up to my parents lovingly, and with a great deal of respect. I appreciated their sacrifice to immigrate to the U.S., and how hard they had to work to support four kids. This was no easy task, as they did not speak English. I tried to be the "good son" per Chinese cultural norms.

As an adult, I have become estranged from my surviving parent (my mom) and my three siblings. I spent the first thirty years of my life trying to get the approval of my parents and family, something that they made clear they would never give me. They used my trying to be a good son, and my desire for their validation to be manipulative, controlling, and unnecessarily cruel. I was constantly pressured to do things I didn't want to. Most of these things were arbitrary and didn't affect them at all. They just wanted complete control over me. It brought my mother immense happiness and joy to have me choose unhappiness for her. They would then berate me for choosing what they decided for me.

"We didn't pressure you."

"You chose it yourself."

"No one held a gun to your head."

Basically I was a "dick", "faggot", or "pussy" if I didn't do what they said, and when I did do it, I was a "dick", "faggot", or "pussy" anyway. If anything, things got worse when I did what they decided. It just really isn't difficult to pressure a child into doing things they don't want to.

My mother is a narcissist and is the reason my siblings and I can't stand each other. There are so many stories, but there are 3 in particular I would like to share:

1. When I was 13, and graduating junior high, they wanted me to go to a private parochial high school. I, of course, did not want to go. Like all kids, I wanted to go to high school with the friends I was growing up with. Then the whole family got involved in pressuring me to go. My mother, three siblings, and extended family (aunts and uncles) were constantly berating, bitching, and whining at me to do what they ordered me to do. After WEEKS of unrelenting pressure, I caved and agreed to go. What I mean by pressure is constantly being yelled at in private and public, at restaurants, and family gatherings. Immediately after I agreed to go, they said, "We didn't pressure you to do this. You wanted to go". This followed by constant bitching about how much it cost, and the suffering this was causing. I, of course, tried to stand up for myself and replied with, "Fine I won't go then." This was met with yelling and screaming about what an ingrate I was, and

how I didn't appreciate their sacrifices. It was a pathetic attempt at standing up for myself, but it was a 13-year-old trying to stand up to the whole family, including extended family while being yelled at. I was a "dick", "faggot", or "pussy" for not doing what they wanted, and a bigger "dick", "faggot", or "pussy" for doing it.

2. I have three siblings - an older brother, and two older sisters. Brother is the oldest, and the "Golden Child". He works and brings home money to support the family. He is suffering and sacrificing. I supported the family for several years on my own, yet I was a "dick", "faggot", or "pussy" for doing it. My siblings are 2 years apart and planned. I was born 4 years apart from the closest sibling, a mistake. I am constantly reminded of this. My sisters being four and six years older than me used to physically abuse me for fun. I would tell my parents about the physical abuse and get yelled at for it. If my parents were around when it happened, I would scream, crying for their help. They would then berate me for bothering them and tell me that they weren't sure if I was a boy or girl because I was always crying. My siblings would all be laughing at this and would join in on the lecture about what a "dick", "faggot", or "pussy" I was.

3. This wasn't isolated to just my siblings. Anyone could treat me poorly, and I would get yelled at for defending myself. Car salesman, sister's boyfriend, security guard

who insulted my dad. My sister's boyfriend
used to join in on the fun of tormenting me. He
would fuck with me until I cried, and my sister
and him would laugh about it. She would then
go tell my other siblings, and they would laugh
about it. She would then go tell my mom about
what I said to her boyfriend. I would then get
yelled at by my mom for defending myself. For
example, my sister's boyfriend used to call my
mom a slanted-eye whore. I would tell him,
"Fuck your wetback. Get the fuck out." I would
get slapped around and would cry. Then my
siblings would laugh about me crying, and then
laugh again when my mother was yelling at
me. My mother would never let an opportunity
to put me down publicly go by.

Life was definitely a struggle. What I learned is
that not everyone is deserving of a space in
your heart. There is nothing you can do to
make someone love you, care about you, or
even treat you with the smallest amount of
common decency. I have learned to be careful
with who I let into my heart, who I care about,
and who I try to help.

I made a conscious effort to not be like them. I
went to therapy and could probably use more. I
have worked hard to not be like them and
recognize the people with golden hearts. I am
affectionate to my nephews and friends, who
are the only semblance of family I have. I try to
make sure they know I love them. I say, "I love
you", which is something I never heard from my

family. I am generous with my friends, and never expect anything back, or guilt them about it. I do not waste time trying to work things out with someone who does not have the emotional capability to be a decent person. I have learned to be fiercely independent, and count on myself. I take total responsibility for my life, and the results of my decisions and actions. The downside is I have a really difficult time asking for help.

On the other hand, as you may have noticed, I didn't mention my father previously. My father was a traditional Asian male and father. He was stoic. He never pressured me, or any of my siblings, to do anything. He left the child rearing to my mother. There were probably only half a dozen times where he expressed anger towards me. His emotional range was very limited - anger and disapproval. I think I hugged my father three times from when I was a teenager until he passed away in 1995. I know so little of my father, and wish I knew more. I remember trying to have a conversation with him in high school, and he just looked annoyed. While he was unaffectionate, he was not abusive. I guess I prefer to be left alone than to be abused.

My father liked fireworks, and we would set off fireworks every 4th of July. One year, we were having financial difficulty, and my mom said we can skip fireworks this year. My dad said, "No, Bogin's not going to miss fireworks this year." This was a private conversation between my mother and father that was told to me later. Though he didn't say much to me and was unaffectionate towards me, this would be the best example of how he showed love. He never came to me and guilted me about it nor bitched about what a sacrifice it was. My mother would have tormented me over it.

My father never sought recognition for anything he was supposed to do. He didn't feel he was special because he worked hard to support his family. Now, I also don't seek validation for the things that I should do. Go to college, manage, and develop my career - these are things you're supposed to do. It doesn't make you a victim or hero for doing it. I also do not think anyone owes me anything except common decency.

I have gone noncontact with my family, so I have a pretty good idea about what my life is like without them. I am no longer bitched at for everything I do. I am no longer guilted for just existing. I do what they say, "dick", "faggot", or "pussy"; I don't do what they say, "dick", "faggot", or "pussy". I haven't spoken to my mother since 2003 and my siblings since 2005. My nephews are the only relatives I keep in touch with. I am the happiest I have ever been. I live with every one of my decisions. I take aggressive responsibility for my successes and fuckups.

My parents were hard workers and suffered in silence, like many immigrants working unskilled labor. We were poor, and I had a job since I was 11. By the time I was 13, I didn't take lunch money from them and bought my own school clothes. I have always worked hard and put my career first. This has helped me, as I don't have a family to fall back on. If things went to shit for me, I would be homeless, except for the fact that I would be willing to do unskilled labor to survive. I would downsize, stop going out, live in a shittier neighborhood, and rebuild if I need to. When I went no contact with my family, I was broken. They used to control me through my finances. I was giving them 75% of my take home pay. I have learned to persevere through difficult times, and work to get out of the hole and rebuild. Working hard through everything was one of the lessons I took from my parents.

If I would have one more day with my father, well, this is a tough question as the father I know wouldn't have much to say to me. But if we were granted an extra day knowing it was an extra day, I think he would let me know that he loved me and try to impart knowledge that would help me in my adult life. I can't recall him ever saying he loved me.

In this day and age, having children is a choice and a gift. No one asks to be born. It seems like some parents have children just so they can bitch at them. Other parents have children as fashion accessories to validate their own existence. Then they get mad when their child doesn't want to be a doctor, lawyer, etc., because they think it makes them look bad. Parents are not the main characters in their child's story. I have heard horror stories about mothers ruining their son/daughter's wedding by making it about them. Fathers ruin their sons trying to make them athletes, doctors, lawyers., etc. Children are to be loved, raised, and developed so they go through this journey called life armed with the emotional wherewithal to handle difficulties thrown at them, and to achieve some semblance of happiness and success, however they define it.

~ ~
~ ~

I'm so grateful for all my guest authors. I know that some of them have never told anyone how they feel through all these years. Sharing how one feels is part of the healing and the growth.

Throughout history the elders would always share their stories to their tribes. In these modern times, we have forgotten how important storytelling is for our development as individuals. From grandparents, family members, teachers, and our parents, talking about what humanity has gone through is so important. And I pray for individuals like my guest writers to keep having the love and courage to talk about their stories, good and bad, to teach and heal our future generations.

"Awareness is observation without choice, condemnation, or justification. Awareness is silent observation from which there arises understanding without the experiencer and the experienced. In this awareness, which is passive, the problem or the cause is given an opportunity to unfold itself and so give its full significance. In awareness there is no end in view to be gained, and there is no becoming, the 'me' and the 'mine' not being given the continuity."

-Jiddu Krishnamurti

Chapter SEVEN

The Gift

I decided to write this book because I finally decided to give myself love and forgiveness and get my self-power back. I have lived a life through fear, and I mean all sorts of fears. From having this crazy fear of having the lights off at night, stage fright, not being loved and seen, body shame, to the fear of never achieving my dreams, generational fear, and fears that I didn't understand "The Why".

There's a famous Buddha quote: "Holding onto anger is like drinking poison and expecting the other person to die." I realized that it may seem like a silly saying, but it's very factual. In all stories, the only one that gets hurt is just oneself: YOU. All these fears that we encounter, they are all real for you, and no one else. Even at my age, in my late 30s, when I sleep over at my friends' houses, I leave the lights on. Do I let fears dictate my life? No! I do my best, depending on how I'm feeling that day. Sometimes I'm better at overcoming the fear, and I turn off the lights.

No one is perfect at all. We are all perfectly IMPERFECT, and that allows us to keep on growing, keep discovering things that we like and dislike, and keep on discovering that every sunset is different and has its own uniqueness.

Know that, as humans, it is always easy to fall into that negative mental loop. We all do it - even that one person that you know that is always super happy with a very crazy and huge smile. Yes, it happens to that one too. We all have continuous negative thoughts about how we look, how we talk, how we perform at work or school, or in our relationships. We might not feel seen or loved or whatever. And this loop that I'm talking about pretty much is like a broken record. It keeps going and going for a day or many days, maybe telling you how dumb you looked yesterday at your work presentation, and that little statement creates a big loop and gets bigger and bigger. The little voice in your head keeps narrating the whole scenario over and over. And I repeat, we ALL do it! The point here is how often or how long did you let this loop go?

Live one day at a time and use all your tools - all those tools that you have collected from Mom, Dad, and all the mentors along your way that have helped you. Move on from that loop. Most of our adult problems come from our childhood traumas. They can be very little, such as your brother scaring you with a dead spider, or others may be more serious, like unfortunately, when kids get physically and mentally abused. I'm not trying to minimize your experiences at all; I'm just trying to shine some light on YOU, the HERO of your life's story. All those traumas that we go through can't get erased from our minds, hearts, and souls, but we can leave them there at that exact moment when they happen - 5 years ago, 10 years ago, or whatever time it was when someone hurt us. Being that our parents are the individuals closest to us, we tend to blame them with good or bad reason. Yet, they might not be guilty at all. Acknowledging what happened to us is the first step to healing.

For me, acknowledging my parents as my greatest teachers, gave me a perspective on them too. It came with traumas - unresolved feelings, childhood trauma, and generational trauma. And well, no one gave them a manual to know how to raise you and love you and see you. Our parents were given to us with an invisible huge badge tied from their heart.

They are, whether you want to admit or not, the base for the better you. If they gave you nothing, you definitely learned that there are better ways to go about life out there. If they gave you everything, you most likely would try to do the best with all those teachings. Even when your parents were not there or they abandoned you, you turned that into the lesson of perhaps never to leave anyone like that. And even in the worst moments, when life took your parents too soon, the hidden lesson of discovering who you really are, is the gift from our deceased parents.

The following are some of the questions my guest writers answered for this book. Here are my answers:

How would you describe your parents as you were younger and now?

As you guys might remember, Dad was always fun and passed aways at a very young age.

Mom I used to not like much when I was younger. She demanded too much from me and never made me feel loved or seen. Later on I learned that Mom was doing her best and we are now best friends. I enjoy her very much - her stories, her knowledge and even when we talk about things that we don't agree on. We know that the bond that we have is stronger than any silly disagreement. As for Dad, I wish I would've known him, the real him.

Which parent was the one that has made you suffer/struggle the most and tell me the first story that comes to mind?

For me, it was Mom. She was so harsh on us and had very little patience. I remember once I told her to leave me alone and that she was not the boss of me. I got spanked hard for that.

Years later did you learn anything or gain a different perspective from those not so pleasant moments? If so, tell how those lessons have molded you as a person and in your personal life.

Getting spanked frequently as a kid - with a shoe, iron cable and/or metal hangers - really taught me that perhaps violence was not the best way to deal with kids. Love perhaps was a better way about it. Now that I'm a bit older and I have worked on myself and am healing, I do see Mom with different eyes. I can see her pain and frustration to raise 3 little kids on her own. I work to be compassionate towards everyone as we don't know what journeys and pain other people are going through.

Which parent was the one that has made you happy the most (can be the same parent if that applies), and tell me the first story that comes to mind?

As a child, living with mom was like walking on shells, and I don't remember a happy moment. But last year, she was telling me a story: She went to the beach and right next to the court (beach volleyball), she saw a guy getting ready to play. He put on his sunscreen, his UV long sleeved t-shirt, sunglasses, and sand socks. He also had with him like a sack of pro-volleyball balls. Being that my mom had played volleyball since she was little all the way to college and in her adult life (she even played in tournaments), she was so excited to see this guy play. She said, "I mean he looked like such a pro." He asked his friends, who were pros, to let him in. He went in to play, and he did play but not at the pro level she expected. We were laughing so hard, my mom even thought this guy was the coach or something. I know it was a silly story, but it just made us laugh so hard that we were crying.

Dad was just fun to be around, especially when he used to take us to the water park. We never wanted to leave, so he would always scream,

"You are going to turn into a fish, get out of the water!!" I laughed every time.

Life is a roller coaster. Whether you have hated your parents or loved them, for a quick minute imagine your life without them. How does that look? We always feel like our life is the worst or that we have the worst parents and siblings and that everyone's life is so much better. I think as time goes by, I see that rollercoaster in a more fun manner. I take breaks, I scream, I laugh, I cry. It has its ups and downs, and I try to see all those as opportunities to be a better me, a better human where I can better serve my community, my friends, and those that I consider my friends.

I mean, no one likes to go through disappointments and heartbreaks, or not feel loved and seen, or not having a job, or a house, or going through the passing of our loved ones. But those are the moments that push us to either dig a bigger hole and stay in the pity party, or to try to slowly come out of that hole better, with a bit more knowledge every time. Life takes us and throws things at us, sometimes great, sometimes hard.

Tell me a story that has impacted you the most, where you held your parents' teachings to go through it.

One thing that I keep with me from Dad that has helped me my whole life is his saying that I can do everything and anything that I want to. Even when I had doubts about myself, I can hear his voice saying that to me. Nothing is impossible, we just need to want it that bad. And Mom taught me that working hard with principles and honesty will take me far.

Life also has funny ways of teaching us things, and the passing of our parents is one of those. If you are one of those kids, if you could have them with you for one more day, what would you tell them to do or not do?

I'm one of those kids who, at a very young age, had to go through the passing of my dad. If I can have him one more day, I would tell him how much I miss him and love him. I would ask him a thousand questions - about what he likes, what he dislikes, and how his parents were with him. I'd ask about his dreams, and I'd ask if he knew love. I would tell him all about my fu*^# k ups and everything that I've been working so hard on for the past years. And finally, I would just hold his hand as long as I could.

And lastly, if right NOW, at this point in your life, you only had a few minutes to tell your parents/foster parents/parent figures anything, whether good or bad, what would that be?

Losing my father was horrible, and the thought of not having Mom after everything we have

now, I'm sure would be a very sad moment.
The passing of someone, whether it is your
parent or other family member or a friend, it will
always be hard. But I know I understand death
in a different way. It is not taboo, and it is not
the end of anyone. It is just a transition of the
physical body into our energy/celestial body. I
will tell Mom that she was my hero and my rock
and that she was my REAL model. I will tell her
that her life was an example to many and that
every single patient she helped was so grateful
for her. She was the best nurse ever.

I would tell her to be happy and that I will hold
her in my heart until my last breath.

-- - -- - - --- - ---   - -- -   -   - --- - ---- - - ----- - ---- --

Answering those questions was a very tough
thing to do, but definitely healing, and I'm sure it
brought awareness, not only to me, but to all
my guest writers.

I can tell you, learning to love my mother again
has been one of the best gifts I have given to
myself.

Knowing where I come from, and the struggles
of my parents, has really shown me all these
perspectives, and that the way I was living was
doing a total disservice for myself.

My quest perhaps was not to go back and dig
for something, but realizing that I was who I

was because of all the situations I had lived
through, for all those roads that I had crossed,
with the people that eventually became friends
and with those friends that became family, and
with all those individuals that we get to call
family, those that sooner or later we realized
that for the most part they won't disappeared
from our lives if we don't want them to. We have
their unconditional presence in our lives.

Give yourself a new light on all your problems
and struggles. Nothing is forever, even your
struggles, God/the universe, however you want
to call it, gives you only what you can handle.

So, chin up! Hating where you came from is not
going to help you but will keep you in the same
state of mind. Each day we get a new chance to
f*^#k things up or make things better, and if it
wasn't enough, you at least did your best.

Our greatest teachers are our parents, as we
are for them. Our parents, for most, are the role
models, but there are also the foster parents,
the aunts and uncles that took the time to see
us, our teachers, friends, and mentors.

We all serve each other, whether we feel like it
or not. All individuals that you have
encountered have made you smile, sad or
impact on you in some way that you will carry
with you in life. I believe that we need to know

the importance of ourselves for this world, our community, and our families. Every time you go out the door, you can change lives for the good or for the bad and being aware of this power makes us more conscious, more whole, as we are part of something bigger than we can imagine.

Our lives are so short. So, get whatever lemons you have and make your lemonade. And if you have nothing, look for those seeds to grow your own tree, to then get your own lemons to make your own lemonade. Take what you have and make the best out of it. Make lemonade, share your lemons, grow your tree, or grow oranges if you don't like lemons. No excuses. No more whining. No more looking at the greener side. No more blaming. No more holding those feelings that don't serve you for your highest good. No more blaming your parents and your upbringing. But better turn all that around, take all that as an opportunity to show you how badass you are. Life is infinite and so are you. You've got this!

Afterword

My intention was to write a book to share my stories and those of anyone out there that trusted me with their family stories and experiences. I felt that it was important to know that I'm not the only one that had mixed feelings towards my parents and family. I believe in the power of storytelling and how we can all change for the better by recognizing that it is not always greener on the other side of the road. We all live a hard life at times in our own feelings and with our own experiences. Also, I wanted to shine a light on all the mentors we encounter in life, directly and indirectly. In reality, it is all about perception, and in order to succeed into our highest self, we must take a 360 degree look at everything that happens to us. It's not about blaming, it's about learning. Some of us choose to learn this sooner than others. There is not a perfect time to start or continue learning, but it is important to keep on learning.

I hope to open your heart and mind about your own life. I hope I planted a seed for you to keep on flourishing for the rest of your life and to keep on changing to better the generations to come.

Sources:

These are books and websites that I referenced for this book and that have informed me and my work to write the book and helped me with self-help:

**Don Miguel Ruiz

The Four Agreements

www.miguelruiz.com

** Keri Norley

The New Wealth: Magnetize Abundance, Hold your Wealth and Leave a Legacy

www.kerinorley.com

** Laura Powers

Healing Powers Podcast

www.laurapowers.net

**Wikipedia

*Super Soul Podcast,

*Don't Keep your Day Job Podcast

Alex's Book List :

The Four Agreements: A Practical Guide to Personal Freedom

The Mastery of Love: A Practical Guide to the Art of Relationship

Toltec Wisdom Book

The Fifth Agreement: A Practical Guide to Self-Mastery

The Voice of Knowledge: A Practical Guide to Inner Peace

The Toltec Art of Life and Death

All those books by Don Miguel Ruiz

The New Wealth: Magnetize Abundance, Hold your Wealth and Leave a Legacy By Keri Norley

The Seat of the Soul by Gay Zukav

The Awakened Family by Shefali Tsabary Ph.D.

The Subtle Art of not giving a F*ck by Mark Manson

Big Magic by Elizabeth Gilbert

All Brene Brown Books

We are Going to Need More Wine by Gabrielle Union

I've Been Thinking by Maria Shriver

Mom Me & Mom by Maya Angelou

Jump by Steve Harvey

You are a Badass by Jen Sincero

What I Know for Sure by Oprah Winfrey

The Last Lecture by Randy Pausch

A New Earth by Eckhart Tolle

Relentless by Tim Grover

The Alchemist by Paulo Coelo

About the Author – Alex Balgood

Alex Balgood is an author, artist, creator, dancer, MLD certified massage therapist, Podcaster, host of Leap of Health Podcast, YouTuber host of Dough Around the World and a life and nutritionist coach.

But before all that, she is a daughter, a sister and a friend.

Grew up in a small town moved to one of the biggest cities in the world LA, California at 15.

Decided it to gave up on her scholarship as an engineer to pursue Art in all forms, Acting, Singing, Painting, Designing, Dancing and Writing.

She has traveled the world to understand humanity better, she understands the importance to see the world, the cultures, the believes, etc.

She is a dreamer and would keep on doing her best to keep on dreaming and to keep on doing to honor her Dad and Mom

www.ingramcontent.com/pod-product-compliance
Lightning Source LLC
Chambersburg PA
CBHW071451130726
47997CB00006B/2315